GOODNIGHT

STORIES FROM THE QURAN FOR KIDS

INTEGRITY   **RESPECT**   **KINDNESS**   **VALUES**

بسم الله الرحمن الرحيم

In the name of Allah, the Most Gracious, the Most Merciful

All praise is due to Allah, the Lord of all worlds. Peace and blessings be upon the final messenger, Prophet Muhammad (SAW), and upon his family and companions.

Esteemed Readers,

Welcome to this curated collection of stories, meticulously crafted to inspire moral integrity, empathy, and kindness in the hearts of our young audience. Rooted in the tapestry of Islamic tradition, these narratives delve into the lives of the Prophets, unraveling timeless lessons that transcend cultural and temporal boundaries.

In the contemporary world we navigate, where challenges are diverse and children encounter a myriad of influences, it becomes imperative to furnish narratives that serve as guiding lights. The stories in this collection are not only meant to captivate young minds but also to instill values that serve as the foundation for character development.

The lives of the Prophets, as depicted in these pages, stand as exemplary models for our youth to emulate. Each narrative unfolds with the intention of fostering a profound connection with moral virtues such as patience, courage, gratitude, and compassion. Through the experiences of these esteemed figures, our aim is to sow the seeds of empathy and kindness, encouraging children to be mindful of their actions and considerate of others.

Interwoven among the prophetic tales are stories that touch on universal themes, illustrating the beauty of friendship, the significance of honesty, and the strength found in unity. These narratives complement the Prophetic stories, reinforcing the overarching message of cultivating a character firmly rooted in virtue.

As parents, educators, and caretakers, we play a pivotal role in shaping the moral compass of the younger generation. It is our sincere hope that this collection becomes a cherished companion in the journey of imparting values that transcend generations. May these stories serve as a source of inspiration, conversation, and reflection within the sacred spaces of homes, schools, and communities.

May Allah, the Most Merciful, bless this endeavor and make these stories a means of instilling enduring virtues in the hearts of our precious children.

Peace and blessings be upon you all.

The Editorial Team

Table of Content

The Life of Prophet Muhammad (SAW): A Source of Mercy for Mankind

Prophet Muhammad (SAW), born in the year 570 CE in Mecca, holds a unique and revered place in Islamic history as the final messenger of Allah and the seal of prophethood. His life, chronicled in the Quran, Hadith, and historical records, reflects a tapestry of honesty, integrity, and trustworthiness from his youth, earning him the honorific title "Al-Amin" (the trustworthy) among his people.

At the age of 40, during a period of contemplation within the Cave of Hira, the angel Jibreel (Gabriel) brought the first revelation from Allah to Muhammad (SAW). Over the subsequent 23 years, the Quran unfolded, providing guidance for all facets of life and addressing challenges confronted by the burgeoning Muslim community.

Persecution in Mecca intensified due to Prophet Muhammad's (SAW) preaching of monotheism and condemnation of idol worship. Undeterred by adversity, he persevered with patience and resilience. In 622 CE, faced with escalating hostility, he and his followers undertook the Hijra, migrating to Medina, marking the inception of the Islamic calendar.

In Medina, Prophet Muhammad (SAW) laid the foundation for a society grounded in justice, compassion, and mutual respect. Serving as a leader, mediator, and judge, he adeptly resolved conflicts and nurtured unity among diverse communities. The Constitution of Medina, a document authored by the Prophet, stands as a milestone in early constitutional history.

Challenges abounded, including battles against those seeking to extinguish Islam, yet Prophet Muhammad (SAW) personified forgiveness and mercy, even extending it to his staunchest adversaries. The conquest of Mecca in 630 CE became a triumph of peace and reconciliation, as the Prophet forgave those who had once persecuted him.

The Night Journey (Isra and Mi'raj), a miraculous event, saw Prophet Muhammad (SAW) leading the believers in prayers at the Al-Aqsa Mosque in Jerusalem before ascending through the heavens. His teachings, encompassing ethics, morality, family matters, commerce, and governance, offered comprehensive guidance for all aspects of life.

In 632 CE, during his farewell pilgrimage, Prophet Muhammad (SAW) delivered a poignant sermon, emphasizing the equality of all Muslims and the sanctity of human life and property. A few months later, he peacefully departed this world in Medina, leaving behind a legacy of compassion, justice, and unwavering devotion to Allah.

Prophet Muhammad (SAW) is venerated as a mercy to mankind, and his life serves as an enduring source of inspiration for millions of Muslims globally. Preserved in the Quran and Hadith, his teachings continue to guide those seeking a life marked by righteousness and compassion.

The legacy of Prophet Muhammad (SAW) continued to illuminate the path of righteousness and compassion long after his departure from this world. His profound teachings resonated through the hearts of his companions and followers, laying the groundwork for an ethical and just society.

Following the demise of the Prophet, his close companion Abu Bakr (RA) assumed the mantle of leadership as the first Caliph. Inheriting the weighty responsibility of guiding the Muslim community, Abu Bakr (RA) faced external threats and internal challenges. Yet, he exemplified the teachings of Prophet Muhammad (SAW) in his humility, justice, and unwavering commitment to Islam.

Under Abu Bakr's (RA) leadership, the nascent Muslim community successfully repelled the apostasy wars and preserved the unity of the Islamic state. His Caliphate was marked by fiscal responsibility, transparency, and a dedication to the welfare of the people, embodying the principles laid down by Prophet Muhammad (SAW).

Following Abu Bakr's (RA) tenure, Umar ibn al-Khattab (RA) assumed leadership, becoming the second Caliph. His governance mirrored the justice and compassion modeled by Prophet Muhammad (SAW). Umar (RA) expanded the Muslim empire, ensuring that the principles of Islam guided administrative decisions and societal welfare.

The succeeding Caliphs, Uthman ibn Affan (RA) and Ali ibn Abi Talib (RA), further upheld the legacy of Prophet Muhammad (SAW). Uthman (RA) facilitated the compilation of the Quran into a standardized text, a project initiated during the time of Abu Bakr (RA). Ali (RA) stood as a paragon of courage and justice, carrying forward the principles of his predecessors.

However, the period following the Rashidun Caliphs witnessed internal divisions within the Muslim community, leading to the emergence of the Umayyad and Abbasid Caliphates. Despite political differences, the teachings of Prophet Muhammad (SAW) remained a unifying force, influencing the scholars, philosophers, and scientists who contributed to the Islamic Golden Age.

During this golden era, Islamic civilization flourished, making significant advancements in various fields, including science, medicine, philosophy, and literature. The scholars of this period, inspired by the ethical teachings of Prophet Muhammad (SAW), played a pivotal role in preserving and transmitting knowledge to subsequent generations.

The spirit of mercy and compassion embodied by Prophet Muhammad (SAW) continued to resonate through the annals of Islamic history. His life, teachings, and exemplary character shaped the narrative of generations to come, leaving an indelible mark on the hearts of millions who continue to draw inspiration from the final messenger of Allah.

As centuries passed, the enduring impact of Prophet Muhammad's (SAW) teachings persisted, transcending geographical boundaries and cultural divides. Islamic civilization, with its rich tapestry of knowledge and values, continued to evolve, contributing to the collective heritage of humanity.

The establishment of renowned Islamic centers of learning, such as the House of Wisdom in Baghdad, became beacons of enlightenment. Scholars from diverse backgrounds convened, translating works from ancient civilizations, preserving knowledge, and expanding the horizons of human understanding. Through these endeavors, the legacy of the Prophet's (SAW) emphasis on seeking knowledge thrived.

In the realms of art, architecture, and literature, Islamic civilization showcased its creativity and ingenuity. The intricate geometric patterns adorning mosques, the poetic expressions of love and spirituality, and the scientific treatises rooted in empirical observation all bore the influence of the ethical principles exemplified by Prophet Muhammad (SAW).

Throughout the ages, the teachings of Islam continued to guide societies in matters of ethics, justice, and compassion. Islamic scholars and jurists, drawing inspiration from the Quran and the Sunnah, developed comprehensive legal frameworks that upheld the rights of individuals and fostered societal harmony.

As empires rose and fell, and as the world underwent various transformations, the life of Prophet Muhammad (SAW) remained a timeless source of guidance. His teachings on social justice, economic equity, and the sanctity of life inspired movements for positive change across diverse cultures and epochs.

In the modern era, the principles of Prophet Muhammad (SAW) continue to be a source of inspiration for Muslims navigating the complexities of the contemporary world. His emphasis on tolerance, diversity, and compassion serves as a compass for those seeking a balanced and ethical approach to the challenges of the 21st century.

The Prophet's (SAW) legacy endures not only in religious practices but also in the hearts and minds of millions who strive to emulate his virtues. His life continues to be a source of mercy for mankind, a beacon illuminating the path towards a just, compassionate, and morally upright society. As we reflect on the legacy of Prophet Muhammad (SAW), we find timeless wisdom that resonates across the ages, offering a roadmap for individuals and communities striving for excellence in both spiritual and worldly pursuits.

Prophet Adam and the Garden of Obedience: Redemption and Divine Mercy

In the distant past, Allah, in His infinite wisdom, created the first human, Prophet Adam (AS), with meticulous care, fashioning him with His own hands. With a divine breath, Allah animated Adam, infusing him with life. Placed in the enchanting expanse of Paradise, Adam found himself surrounded by the splendors of a garden that catered to his every need.

However, Adam's existence in Paradise was not solitary. Allah, in His benevolence, created Hawwa (Eve) as a companion for him. Together, they enjoyed the tranquility of Paradise, basking in the magnificence of Allah's creation. Amidst this bliss, Allah, in His wisdom, set forth a single restriction—they were forbidden to partake of the fruit from a specific tree.

Yet, the harmony in Paradise was disrupted when Iblis (Satan) insidiously whispered to Adam and Hawwa, cunningly attempting to lead them astray. He painted the forbidden tree as irresistibly enticing, and sadly, Adam and Hawwa succumbed to the temptation, consuming the forbidden fruit.

Recognizing their lapse, they felt a profound sense of remorse and turned to Allah in sincere repentance. In His boundless mercy, Allah forgave them, imparting words of forgiveness and providing guidance for their earthly sojourn.

Adam and Hawwa were subsequently appointed as Allah's vicegerents on Earth, entrusted with representing Him. They became the progenitors of the entire human race, marking the inception of humanity.

The tale of Prophet Adam conveys profound lessons on the significance of obedience to Allah, the repercussions of disobedience, and the unfathomable mercy bestowed upon those who earnestly repent for their transgressions. It serves as a timeless narrative, guiding humanity toward the path of righteousness and highlighting the boundless mercy of the Creator.

As Adam and Hawwa descended from the heavenly abode to Earth, they embarked on a journey marked by challenges and trials. Settling on Earth, they began to experience the vast spectrum of human emotions, relationships, and the cycles of life.

Their progeny multiplied, and each successive generation faced the complexities of existence. The narrative of Adam's family unfolds with tales of sacrifice, sibling rivalry, and the eventual guidance of prophetic wisdom passed down from generation to generation.

One significant episode in their lineage is the story of the sons of Adam, where envy led to a tragic event. The elder son, Qabil (Cain), out of jealousy, took the life of his younger brother Habil (Abel). This grievous incident became a profound lesson, illustrating the destructive consequences of envy and the sanctity of human life.

In the midst of these challenges, Allah continued to send prophets to guide humanity back to the straight path. The story of Adam's family became a tapestry of lessons on repentance, forgiveness, and the enduring hope for divine mercy. The subsequent prophets in their lineage, including Nuh (Noah), Ibrahim (Abraham), Musa (Moses), and Isa (Jesus), each carried forward the divine message of monotheism and moral conduct.

The story of Adam and his descendants stands as a testament to the resilience of the human spirit and the unending mercy of Allah. Through trials, tribulations, and moments of redemption, humanity's journey unfolded, guided by the divine wisdom revealed to prophets.

As we reflect on the narrative of Prophet Adam (AS) and his progeny, we glean insights into the human condition, the consequences of choices, and the ever-present opportunity for repentance and divine mercy. The story resonates as a beacon of hope, inviting individuals to turn back to Allah, seek forgiveness, and strive for a life aligned with righteousness and obedience to the Creator.

In the course of time, the divine saga continued with the unfolding stories of subsequent prophets, each entrusted with a unique mission to guide humanity back to the path of obedience and righteousness.

Prophet Nuh (Noah), a descendant of Adam, emerged as a pivotal figure in this grand narrative. Confronted with the moral decay of his people, he was chosen by Allah to deliver a powerful message of repentance and divine obedience. Despite facing relentless opposition and ridicule, Prophet Nuh (AS) persevered for centuries, embodying the virtue of patience as he built the ark to save the believers and the animal kingdom from the impending flood.

The baton of prophethood was then passed to the righteous Prophet Ibrahim (Abraham), another esteemed descendant of Adam. His unwavering faith, symbolized by his willingness to sacrifice his beloved son at the command of Allah, exemplified the pinnacle of submission. Ibrahim's legacy extended through his sons, Isma'il (Ishmael) and Ishaq (Isaac), both of whom were chosen as prophets to continue the divine mission.

The story of Prophet Musa (Moses) unfolded, depicting the trials of Bani Israel (Children of Israel) and their liberation from oppression. Musa's leadership showcased the importance of justice, resilience, and adherence to divine guidance, offering profound lessons for generations to come.

Prophet Isa (Jesus), another luminary in the lineage of Adam, was born miraculously to Maryam (Mary). His life was a testament to divine mercy, as he healed the sick, gave sight to the blind, and preached love and compassion. His mission, intricately connected to the overarching message of monotheism, paved the way for the final prophet, Muhammad (SAW).

The culmination of prophethood occurred with the advent of Prophet Muhammad (SAW), the seal of the prophets and a mercy to mankind. His teachings, encapsulated in the Quran, harmonized the divine messages conveyed by his predecessors. The stories of Adam, Nuh, Ibrahim, Musa, Isa, and others became integral components of the collective guidance for humanity.

As we traverse the annals of prophethood, the saga of Prophet Adam and his descendants stands as a foundational chapter. It intertwines with subsequent narratives, forming a cohesive tapestry that underscores the divine plan for humanity's guidance, redemption, and eventual return to the Creator. These stories, echoing through the corridors of time, beckon individuals to reflect on their own journeys, seek repentance, and embrace the boundless mercy that awaits those who turn to Allah with sincerity.

Khalilullah - Prophet Ibrahim (AS): Allah's Beloved Companion

In the ancient land of Mesopotamia, a man named Ibrahim (AS) resided, known for his wisdom, kindness, and steadfast devotion to the one true God, Allah.

Ibrahim (AS) grew up amidst a society steeped in the worship of idols crafted from wood and stone. Yet, from a young age, he felt an unshakeable connection to the unseen Creator. Gazing upon the vastness of the heavens and the earth, he discerned the presence of a singular, omnipotent God who had crafted all existence.

As Ibrahim (AS) matured, he encountered fierce opposition from his people, who vehemently rejected his belief in a solitary God. Undeterred by pressure and even threats, Ibrahim (AS) remained resolute in his faith. In a bold move, he decided to confront the falsehood of the idols.

Under the cover of night, when the city slumbered, Ibrahim (AS) entered the temple housing the idols. With unwavering determination, he shattered all the idols, leaving only one intact, with the broken pieces at its feet. The following morning, when the people discovered the scene, their rage was palpable.

The city leaders, furious over Ibrahim's (AS) actions, devised a punishment. Amassing wood, they erected an immense fire. Ibrahim (AS) was cast into the flames, yet miraculously, by the will of Allah, the fire transformed into a cool and serene refuge, sparing Ibrahim (AS) from harm.

Despite this miraculous intervention, Ibrahim (AS) faced more tribulations. Allah subjected him to challenging trials, one of which was the command to sacrifice his cherished son, Isma'il (AS). Both father and son, ready to submit to Allah's will, prepared for the sacrifice. Yet, before the act, Allah, pleased with their unwavering obedience, provided a ram as a substitute for the sacrifice.

Throughout his life, Ibrahim (AS) dedicated himself to disseminating the message of monotheism and surrender to the one true God. Revered as "Khalilullah," the Friend of Allah, his narrative imparts profound lessons about steadfast faith, championing righteousness, and the limitless mercy of Allah. Ibrahim (AS) serves as an eternal example of devotion and submission, reminding believers of the boundless compassion that emanates from their Creator.

As Ibrahim (AS) continued his journey as "Khalilullah," the Friend of Allah, his life unfolded as a saga of unwavering devotion and submission to the divine will.

One of the pivotal moments in Ibrahim's (AS) life was the divine command to construct the Kaaba, the sacred house of worship in Mecca. Alongside his son Isma'il (AS), Ibrahim (AS) raised the foundations of the Kaaba, laying the cornerstone for the holiest sanctuary in Islam. Their joint efforts, marked by divine guidance, became a symbol of unity, devotion, and the eternal bond between a father and his righteous son.

The legacy of Ibrahim (AS) extended through the generations as Isma'il (AS) became a prophet in his own right, carrying the torch of monotheism. The city of Mecca, once a desolate valley, became a sanctuary for pilgrims from all corners of the globe, a testament to the enduring impact of Ibrahim's (AS) devotion to Allah.

In his later years, Ibrahim (AS) prayed for his descendants to be bestowed with prophethood. Allah answered his prayer, and from his lineage emerged numerous prophets, including Ya'qub (Jacob), Yusuf (Joseph), Musa (Moses), and Isa (Jesus). The prophetic lineage traced back to Ibrahim (AS) served as a continuous source of divine guidance for humanity.

The fervent supplications of Ibrahim (AS) and his wife Sarah (AS) were answered with the miraculous birth of their son Ishaq (Isaac). The divine covenant with Ibrahim (AS) ensured that his righteous descendants would receive divine guidance and blessings, a promise that reverberates through the Abrahamic religions.

Ibrahim (AS) continued to demonstrate exemplary hospitality, compassion, and generosity. His encounters with travelers and guests, including the angelic visitation in the form of guests, exemplified the virtues of welcoming strangers and displaying kindness—a practice highly emphasized in Islam.

In his final moments, Ibrahim (AS) left behind a legacy that transcends time and space. His unwavering faith, epitomized by the title "Khalilullah," serves as a timeless inspiration for believers navigating the complexities of life. The rituals of Hajj, performed by millions of Muslims annually, stand as a living testimony to the enduring influence of Ibrahim's (AS) devotion and submission to Allah.

As believers reflect on the life of Ibrahim (AS), they find in his story a profound illustration of trust, sacrifice, and unyielding faith—a legacy eternally etched in the pages of divine history. The Friend of Allah continues to guide and inspire hearts, reminding humanity of the boundless mercy and compassion of the Creator.

As the sands of time drifted, Ibrahim (AS) embraced the twilight of his life with grace and wisdom. His role as the patriarch of prophethood left an indelible mark on the spiritual tapestry of humanity.

One of Ibrahim's (AS) last and most significant contributions was the establishment of the sacred ritual of Stoning the Devil during Hajj. This symbolic act, where pilgrims cast stones at pillars representing Satan, commemorates Ibrahim's steadfastness in resisting the devil's temptations during his journey.

The legacy of Ibrahim (AS) endured through the resilience of his descendants and the flourishing of monotheism. The Children of Israel, stemming from his grandson Ya'qub (AS), carried the torch of divine guidance. The Abrahamic connection solidified, intertwining the destinies of his progeny with the broader narrative of prophethood.

In Islam, Ibrahim's (AS) legacy reverberates in the call to prayer (Adhan), where his unwavering belief in the oneness of Allah is proclaimed. The annual celebration of Eid al-Adha commemorates Ibrahim's (AS) willingness to sacrifice his son for the sake of Allah, emphasizing the values of obedience, sacrifice, and trust.

As believers circumambulate the Kaaba during Hajj, they retrace the footsteps of Ibrahim (AS) and his family, reaffirming their submission to the divine. The rituals echo the unity and equality intrinsic to Ibrahim's (AS) vision for the sanctified sanctuary.

The narrative of Ibrahim (AS) is not confined to the pages of history; it breathes life into the moral fabric of Islamic teachings. His unwavering trust in Allah, his hospitality to strangers, and his commitment to justice continue to inspire generations to strive for righteousness.

The title "Khalilullah," the Friend of Allah, encapsulates the profound relationship Ibrahim (AS) cultivated with the Creator. His life serves as a beacon, guiding humanity toward humility, gratitude, and an unwavering connection with the Divine.

As believers reflect on the saga of Ibrahim (AS), they find not only a historical account but a timeless source of wisdom and guidance. The Friend of Allah remains eternally embedded in the hearts of those who seek inspiration, mercy, and divine companionship on their journey through life.

The Story of Prophet Yusuf (AS): Endurance in the Face of Betrayal

Prophet Yusuf (AS), the son of Prophet Ya'qub (Jacob), was gifted with unparalleled beauty and wisdom, a blessing that stirred envy within the hearts of his brothers. Driven by jealousy, they hatched a sinister plan to eliminate him and presented a false narrative to their father, Prophet Ya'qub, claiming that a wolf had devoured Yusuf. The grief-stricken father mourned the loss of his beloved son, unaware of the deceit that had transpired.

In reality, Yusuf found himself cast into a well by his own kin. However, this was only the beginning of a remarkable journey guided by divine providence. A passing caravan discovered him and transported him to Egypt, where he became a commodity in the slave market. Despite the myriad trials that awaited him, including false accusations and unjust imprisonment, Yusuf clung steadfastly to his faith, undeterred by the hardships that befell him.

Renowned for his extraordinary ability to interpret dreams, Yusuf's reputation reached the court of the Egyptian ruler. Even in the face of temptation, when the ruler's wife sought to seduce him, Yusuf chose incarceration over succumbing to sin, affirming his unwavering commitment to righteousness.

Within the confines of prison, Yusuf continued to showcase his wisdom by interpreting the dreams of his fellow inmates. His reputation as a dream interpreter eventually reached the ruler, who sought Yusuf's counsel. Not only did Yusuf interpret the ruler's dream, but he also prophesied a severe famine. Impressed by his insight, the ruler appointed Yusuf to a position of great authority, entrusting him with significant responsibilities.

Meanwhile, back in Canaan, Yusuf's brothers experienced the harsh consequences of the famine and journeyed to Egypt seeking sustenance. Unaware that they were dealing with their estranged brother, they encountered Yusuf, leading to a poignant reunion marked by divine justice and mercy. In an act of profound forgiveness, Yusuf pardoned his brothers, who, in turn, repented for their past transgressions.

The family of Prophet Ya'qub was joyously reunited in Egypt, and Yusuf's elevated position enabled him to provide abundantly for them during the trying times of famine. The tale of Prophet Yusuf (AS) stands as a testament to the enduring themes of betrayal, resilience, and divine redemption, underscoring the ultimate triumph of righteousness and forgiveness over deceit and envy.

The narrative of Prophet Yusuf (AS) unfolds as a tapestry woven with threads of betrayal, resilience, and divine redemption. Following the poignant reunion with his brothers and the joyous gathering of Prophet Ya'qub's family in Egypt, the saga of Yusuf continued to resonate with profound lessons.

Elevated to a position of great authority in the Egyptian court, Yusuf wielded his power with justice and compassion. As the famine persisted, Yusuf's foresight and planning during times of abundance allowed Egypt to weather the storm, becoming a refuge for those seeking sustenance.

The reunion with his brothers brought forth a pivotal moment of forgiveness and reconciliation. Yusuf, embodying the divine attributes of mercy and compassion, reassured his brothers that there was no blame upon them. Their past actions, driven by envy and betrayal, were transformed into a catalyst for spiritual growth and repentance.

The family of Prophet Ya'qub (AS) flourished in the land of Egypt under the care of Yusuf. The narrative echoes the divine principle of redemption, illustrating how trials and tribulations can lead to profound transformations and the eventual triumph of goodness over adversity.

As Yusuf's story reaches its zenith, the threads of betrayal that once threatened to unravel the fabric of his life are now woven into a pattern of divine wisdom. The resilience displayed by Yusuf throughout his journey becomes a timeless lesson for believers facing trials, encouraging them to endure with patience and trust in Allah's plan.

The enduring legacy of Prophet Yusuf (AS) extends beyond the pages of history, offering a beacon of hope for those navigating the complexities of life. His unwavering commitment to righteousness, forgiveness, and trust in Allah serves as an inspiration for believers striving to navigate the twists and turns of their own journeys.

The tale of Prophet Yusuf (AS) remains a source of reflection, inviting individuals to examine their own lives in light of divine guidance. Through the prism of betrayal and resilience, believers find solace in the recognition that, ultimately, Allah's plan encompasses both trials and triumphs, weaving a narrative that leads to redemption and divine mercy.

Musa (AS): Embarking on the Divine Mission and the Journey of Exodus

Centuries ago, in the heart of Egypt, a time of deep oppression cast its shadow over the land. The Children of Israel, descendants of the honorable Prophet Yaqub (Jacob), found themselves ensnared in the cruel clutches of a Pharaoh who not only oppressed them but also denied the existence of the one true God.

Into this bleak existence emerged a glimmer of hope—Prophet Musa (AS). Born during a time when the Pharaoh, alarmed by a prophecy foretelling his downfall at the hands of a child, ordered the ruthless extermination of all newborn males, Musa's mother, inspired by divine guidance, set him adrift in a small basket upon the Nile.

Destined by Allah's divine plan, the basket drifted into the very palace of the Pharaoh, who, surprisingly, chose to raise the child as his own. As Musa matured, he became acutely aware of his divine calling—to liberate his people from the shackles of oppression and guide them toward the worship of the singular, Almighty God.

Equipped with miraculous signs bestowed upon him by Allah, Musa confronted the Pharaoh, urging him to recognize the oneness of God and release the Children of Israel. Yet, the Pharaoh, blinded by his arrogance, adamantly resisted and questioned Musa's authority.

The divine narrative unfolded with a series of extraordinary miracles. Musa's staff transformed into a serpent, his hand emitted a radiant light, and rivers turned into blood—each miraculous sign aimed at persuading the obstinate Pharaoh to submit to God's will.

Despite witnessing these awe-inspiring miracles, the Pharaoh persisted in his defiance. Finally, Allah decreed a pivotal moment—the parting of the Red Sea. As the Children of Israel, led by Musa, approached the sea with the relentless Pharaoh's army in pursuit, Musa struck the sea with his staff. Miraculously, the waters parted, revealing a dry path for the Israelites to traverse safely.

However, in their unyielding arrogance, the Pharaoh and his army pursued into the parted sea. The waters, obedient to the divine command, closed in, submerging the oppressors and vindicating the faith of Musa and his people.

The saga of Musa (AS) stands as an indomitable testament to the resilience of faith, the consequences of unchecked arrogance, and the ultimate triumph of justice over oppression. Musa's steadfast commitment to his divine mission and the miraculous events that surrounded the liberation of the Children of Israel continue to resonate, inspiring believers to persevere in the face of adversity and affirming the certainty of victory for those who uphold righteousness.

The journey of Prophet Musa (AS) unfolded as a divine epic, weaving together the threads of faith, courage, and the eventual liberation of the oppressed. The narrative deepens as Musa (AS) leads the Children of Israel through the wilderness, navigating both the physical and spiritual challenges that lay ahead.

Guided by divine revelation, Musa (AS) ascended Mount Sinai to receive the Tablets of the Law (Torah) from Allah. The commandments etched on the sacred tablets became the cornerstone of moral and ethical guidance for the Children of Israel, setting forth principles that transcended time and space.

During Musa's (AS) absence, some among the Children of Israel succumbed to the allure of idol worship, fashioning a golden calf in disobedience to the divine commandments. Musa, upon returning, confronted his people with righteous indignation, admonishing them for their transgressions. Yet, in his heart, Musa harbored compassion and sought Allah's forgiveness for his people.

The journey of the Children of Israel continued, marked by trials and tribulations. Divine sustenance, in the form of manna and quails, descended from the heavens, ensuring their physical nourishment. However, the spiritual journey demanded steadfastness and unwavering faith.

Musa (AS) encountered numerous challenges as he led his people through the vast wilderness. Water scarcity, oppressive enemies, and internal dissension tested the resolve of the Children of Israel. Yet, through each trial, Musa's leadership remained a beacon of guidance, and Allah's mercy provided miraculous solutions.

The journey reached its culmination as the Children of Israel approached the Promised Land—Canaan. Musa, in anticipation of the fulfillment of the divine promise, dispatched scouts to survey the land. However, the majority returned with apprehension, expressing doubt in their ability to conquer the formidable inhabitants.

As a consequence of their lack of faith, Allah decreed that the Children of Israel would wander in the wilderness for forty years, with only the younger generation being permitted to enter the Promised Land. This period served as a purgation, purifying the community and instilling a generation with a renewed commitment to Allah.

The narrative of Musa (AS) underscores the intricate relationship between faith, divine guidance, and the consequences of straying from the path of righteousness. His legacy resonates as a timeless source of inspiration, emphasizing the importance of steadfastness, repentance, and reliance on Allah's mercy in the face of life's trials and tribulations. The journey of Musa stands as a testament to the enduring power of faith, unwavering commitment to divine guidance, and the ultimate triumph of those who remain steadfast in their devotion to Allah.

The Story of Prophet Nuh (AS): Noah's Ark and the Great Flood

In a distant era, during a time when the world teetered on the brink of moral decay, Allah, in His infinite wisdom, selected Prophet Nuh (AS) to be the beacon of guidance for a wayward humanity. Nuh (AS), a paragon of patience and steadfastness, embarked on a divine mission to lead his people away from the perils of polytheism and immoral conduct.

Despite Nuh's (AS) tireless efforts to convey the message of repentance, the people persisted in their disobedience. Their defiance escalated, and the warnings issued by Nuh (AS) were met with scoffs and mockery. Witnessing the unwavering persistence in wickedness, Nuh (AS) turned to Allah, beseeching Him for guidance.

In response, Allah unfolded a celestial plan to salvage the righteous and purify the earth. Nuh (AS) received the command to construct an immense ark—a colossal vessel designed to withstand a cataclysmic flood that would sweep across the lands. The ark, a sanctuary of salvation, would accommodate pairs of every creature, safeguarding them from the impending deluge alongside Nuh (AS) and his faithful followers.

Undeterred by the relentless scorn and ridicule from his people, Prophet Nuh (AS) diligently toiled over many years to complete the monumental ark. Throughout this arduous process, he persisted in calling his community to repentance, hopeful that they might turn back to Allah before the impending divine intervention.

The fateful day arrived when the heavens opened, and subterranean waters surged forth, submerging the earth in a deluge of cleansing proportions. The floodwaters spared only those on the divinely ordained ark. Nuh (AS) and the believers, alongside their animal companions, found refuge under the protective veil of Allah's mercy as the torrential waters purged the world of corruption.

As the receding floodwaters revealed the peaks of Mount Judi, the ark gently settled on its slopes. Prophet Nuh (AS) and his devoted followers disembarked, heralding the dawn of a new era. Allah, in His boundless mercy, vowed never again to unleash such devastation upon the earth, and Nuh (AS) resumed his prophetic mission. Guiding the survivors, he steered them toward lives steeped in piety and gratitude.

The tale of Prophet Nuh (AS) stands as an indelible reminder of the repercussions of disobedience, the vital role of patience in delivering Allah's message, and the encompassing mercy of Allah, which shields those who steadfastly uphold their faith.

The epic saga of Prophet Nuh (AS) unfolds as a timeless parable, illustrating the consequences of moral decay and the redemptive power of divine guidance. Nuh (AS), chosen by Allah as the beacon of patience and steadfastness, embarked on a monumental mission to rescue humanity from the abyss of wickedness.

In the face of relentless defiance and mockery from his people, Nuh (AS) beseeched Allah for guidance, leading to the divine command to construct an extraordinary ark. This colossal vessel, designed under celestial guidance, became the sanctuary for pairs of every creature, preserving the righteous from the impending cataclysmic flood.

Undaunted by the scorn he faced, Nuh (AS) dedicated years to the laborious task of constructing the ark. Throughout this time, he persistently called his community to repentance, hoping for their return to righteousness before divine intervention.

The day of reckoning arrived as the heavens opened, and subterranean waters surged forth, cleansing the earth in a deluge of purifying proportions. The ark, safeguarding Nuh (AS) and the faithful, became a symbol of divine mercy amid the torrential waters that purged the world of corruption.

As the floodwaters receded, revealing the peaks of Mount Judi, the ark gently settled, and Nuh (AS) and his followers disembarked, heralding the dawn of a new era. Allah, in boundless mercy, vowed against such devastation again. Nuh (AS) resumed his prophetic mission, guiding survivors toward lives steeped in piety and gratitude.

The tale of Prophet Nuh (AS) resonates as a poignant reminder of the consequences of disobedience, the enduring importance of patience in delivering Allah's message, and the enveloping mercy that shields those steadfast in their faith. Nuh's (AS) journey echoes through time, inviting reflection on the transformative power of repentance and the boundless mercy that accompanies the steadfast adherence to divine guidance.

Prophet Salih (AS): Facing the Trials of the Thamud People

Prophet Salih (AS) emerged as a beacon of guidance in the midst of the wayward tribe of Thamud, an ancient community steeped in arrogance and corruption. Tasked by Allah to lead them back to the righteous path, Prophet Salih (AS) embarked on a mission to awaken their hearts and souls to the worship of the One true God.

Despite his sincere endeavors, the people of Thamud remained obstinate, obstinately resisting Prophet Salih's (AS) teachings and warnings of impending divine retribution. Their continued defiance paved the way for a cataclysmic event – a formidable earthquake that reverberated through the very core of their once-mighty civilization.

In the aftermath, the remnants of the once-proud Thamud lay in ruin, their opulence and authority reduced to mere dust. The divine punishment, meted out as a consequence of their unchecked arrogance and injustice, stood as a poignant reminder of the perils of straying from the path of righteousness. Prophet Salih (AS), standing resolute amidst the ruins, embodied the unwavering commitment of prophets to conveying the divine message, even in the face of vehement opposition.

The tale of Prophet Salih (AS) and the Thamud people is a poignant narrative echoing through the corridors of time, imparting a profound lesson on the significance of humility, moral uprightness, and the inevitable repercussions of rejecting divine guidance. It serves as a universal parable found in the Quran, illustrating the rise and fall of civilizations hinging on their adherence to or deviation from the principles of justice, monotheism, and ethical conduct. This tale transcends epochs, resonating with timeless wisdom for those who seek to navigate the complex tapestry of human existence.

Prophet Salih (AS) stood as a steadfast guide amidst the decadence of the Thamud tribe, a community entrenched in arrogance and moral decay. Tasked by Allah to lead them back to the path of righteousness, Prophet Salih (AS) embarked on a courageous mission to awaken their hearts to the worship of the One true God.

Despite his sincere efforts, the people of Thamud remained obstinate, rejecting Prophet Salih's (AS) teachings and ignoring his warnings of impending divine retribution. Their unyielding defiance set the stage for a momentous event – a powerful earthquake that shook the foundations of their once-mighty civilization.

In the aftermath, the remnants of Thamud lay in ruins, their former opulence and authority reduced to dust. The divine punishment served as a stark reminder of the consequences of unchecked arrogance and injustice. Prophet Salih (AS), standing resolute amidst the desolation, exemplified the unwavering commitment of prophets to convey the divine message, even in the face of vehement opposition.

The tale of Prophet Salih (AS) and the Thamud people echoes through time as a poignant narrative, imparting a profound lesson on the importance of humility, moral integrity, and the inevitable repercussions of rejecting divine guidance. It serves as a universal parable found in the Quran, illustrating the rise and fall of civilizations based on their adherence to or deviation from the principles of justice, monotheism, and ethical conduct. This tale transcends epochs, resonating with timeless wisdom for those navigating the complex tapestry of human existence.

Prophet Ayub (AS): A Lesson in Enduring Trials

Prophet Ayub (AS), a symbol of unwavering patience and resilience in Islamic tradition, holds a significant place in the hearts of believers. His narrative, drawn from the Quran and authenticated Islamic references, unfolds as a compelling testament to the strength of faith and the rewards bestowed upon those who endure trials with steadfastness.

In a time of prosperity, Prophet Ayub (AS) enjoyed a life filled with righteousness, abundance, and good health, surrounded by a loving family. However, his life took a sudden and profound turn when Allah chose to test him in a manner that would challenge the very essence of his faith.

With relentless trials, Ayub (AS) witnessed the gradual loss of his wealth, his cherished children, and ultimately, his own health. Afflicted by a debilitating illness that caused immense pain, he found himself isolated and abandoned by those who once admired him. Despite the overwhelming suffering, Ayub (AS) clung to his faith, never once expressing discontent with the divine decree.

His wife, burdened by the family's hardships, pleaded with Ayub (AS) to pray for relief. Yet, Ayub (AS) remained resolute, recognizing the trials as tests from Allah. Instead of complaining, he turned to Allah in prayer, seeking His mercy and guidance.

In response to Prophet Ayub's (AS) unwavering patience and heartfelt prayers, Allah, in His boundless mercy, provided a miraculous solution. Ayub (AS) was instructed to strike the ground with his foot, and from that spot emerged a spring of cool, healing water. As Ayub (AS) bathed in this divine water, his health was miraculously restored. Not only did Allah replenish his wealth, but He also bestowed upon Ayub (AS) a new family.

Prophet Ayub's (AS) narrative imparts a profound lesson in patience, trust in Allah, and perseverance amidst adversity. His steadfastness during the most challenging times serves as an enduring inspiration for believers, urging them to endure trials with patience and express gratitude even in adversity.

The timeless story of Prophet Ayub (AS) serves as a beacon of hope, reminding believers that enduring trials with patience and unwavering faith leads to divine rewards. Regardless of the severity of challenges, Ayub's tale assures us that Allah's mercy is ever-present for those who remain devoted and trust in Him during the trials of life.

Prophet Hud's (AS) Divine Revelation

Chosen by Allah to be a messenger, Prophet Hud (AS) embarked on a divine mission to guide the people of 'Ad, a nation known for their strength and wealth but plagued by arrogance and defiance. The once-blessed community had deviated from the path of righteousness, succumbing to oppression and idolatry.

Undaunted by the formidable task ahead, Prophet Hud (AS) tirelessly preached the message of oneness and justice, imploring the people to abandon their wicked ways and return to the true monotheistic faith. Despite his sincere efforts, the people of 'Ad obstinately rejected his teachings, dismissing his warnings and perpetuating corruption and cruelty.

Prophet Hud (AS) faced an uphill battle as he continued to counsel the people, emphasizing the need for repentance and a return to Allah. However, the people's arrogance and defiance prevailed, and they remained oblivious to the impending divine punishment that loomed over them.

In response to their persistent disobedience, Allah decreed a formidable storm to engulf the land of 'Ad. The unleashed tempestuous winds and destructive forces, beyond human comprehension, left the once-prosperous nation in ruins. The devastating calamity served as a stark reminder of the consequences of deviating from the path of righteousness.

Amidst the chaos, Prophet Hud (AS) and those who had believed in his message were spared from the divine retribution. Their unwavering faith and steadfastness in the face of adversity exemplified the significance of heeding divine guidance. The remnants of the once-mighty 'Ad stood as a testament to the destructive nature of arrogance and the inevitable consequences of persisting in wrongdoing.

The story of Prophet Hud (AS) resonates as a poignant lesson, underscoring the importance of humility, repentance, and adherence to divine guidance. It serves as a timeless reminder for believers to remain steadfast in their faith, even when confronted with the storms of life, and to heed the warnings that lead to righteousness and salvation.

Prophet Shuayb (AS): Upholding the Standard of Justice

Prophet Shuayb (AS), recognized as Jethro in biblical tradition, was a venerable messenger chosen by Allah to guide the people of Madyan onto the path of righteousness. His narrative, meticulously detailed in the Quran, unfolds as a compelling account of justice, honesty, and ethical business practices.

The inhabitants of Madyan had strayed from the righteous path, entangled in deceitful trade practices and corrupt dealings. Witnessing their deviance, Allah selected Shuayb (AS) to be their guiding light and reformer. Shuayb (AS) embodied wisdom, integrity, and an unwavering commitment to justice.

Approaching his people with a message of monotheism, Shuayb (AS) implored them to engage in fair business transactions, treating others with justice and honesty. He earnestly reminded them of the repercussions of their unjust actions and appealed to them to fear Allah and repent.

Despite his noble intentions, Shuayb (AS) encountered formidable resistance from his people. Unwilling to forsake their unethical practices, they scorned his message. Nevertheless, Shuayb (AS) remained patient and resolute, steadfastly delivering the divine message entrusted to him.

Persisting in their wrongdoing, the people of Madyan faced the inevitable consequence of Allah's wrath. A formidable earthquake shook the land, serving as an ominous sign of the repercussions of their corruption. The oppressors met their demise, while those who had heeded Shuayb's (AS) message found refuge from the divine punishment.

The story of Prophet Shuayb (AS) serves as a poignant illustration of the pivotal role justice plays in economic dealings. It stands as a timeless reminder that ethical conduct and righteousness are indispensable for the well-being of society. Shuayb's (AS) unwavering commitment to justice, even in the face of adversity, stands as a beacon of inspiration for believers, emphasizing the profound importance of championing truth and fairness in every facet of life.

The Story of Prophet Lut (AS): Cities Engulfed in Sin

In the ancient city of Sodom, a shadow of moral degradation loomed over its inhabitants, as they immersed themselves in acts of immorality and wickedness. Witnessing this deviance, Allah, in His infinite wisdom and mercy, chose Prophet Lut (AS) as the divine guide to steer the people back onto the path of righteousness.

Prophet Lut (AS), a nephew of the esteemed Prophet Ibrahim (AS), entered Sodom with a solemn message of virtue and monotheism. Despite his sincere efforts, the people of Sodom persisted in their sinful ways, rejecting the divine guidance offered by Allah through His chosen messenger.

In his unwavering commitment to the divine mission, Prophet Lut (AS) warned the people of the impending consequences of their actions. Yet, the residents of Sodom remained obstinate, stubbornly clinging to their immoral practices and rejecting the call to repentance.

In a final plea for their salvation, Prophet Lut (AS) implored the people to abandon their wicked behavior and embrace the worship of the one true God. Tragically, his heartfelt appeals fell on deaf ears, and the people not only refused to reform but also conspired to harm the righteous messenger.

Witnessing the people's persistent disobedience, Allah, in His divine justice, decreed a severe punishment. An angelic messenger was dispatched to Prophet Lut (AS) with a solemn warning and instructions to evacuate the city with his family before the impending catastrophe unfolded.

Prophet Lut (AS) and his faithful followers adhered to the divine command, leaving the doomed cities behind. As the people of Sodom and Gomorrah continued down their path of disobedience, the heavens unleashed a series of earthquakes and a rain of stones, eradicating the sinful cities and their immoral inhabitants.

Prophet Lut (AS) and his family, having heeded Allah's guidance, emerged unscathed from the destruction that befell the sinful cities. The story of Prophet Lut (AS) stands as a profound lesson, illustrating the dire consequences of moral corruption and underscoring the paramount importance of adhering to the righteous path prescribed by Allah. This narrative serves as a timeless reminder of the consequences of straying from divine guidance and the mercy that awaits those who choose repentance and righteousness.

The Tale of Prophet Yunus (AS): A Journey of Repentance and Divine Redemption

Prophet Yunus (AS), also known as Jonah, was chosen by Allah as a messenger to the people of Nineveh. Despite his earnest attempts to guide them toward righteousness, the people remained obstinate in their disobedience and ignored his warnings. Frustrated and thinking his people were beyond salvation, Yunus (AS) left them without waiting for Allah's directive.

Embarking on a sea voyage, Yunus boarded a ship, but Allah, in His infinite wisdom, had other plans for His devoted servant. A violent storm erupted, threatening to consume the vessel. Recognizing the source of the calamity, the crew cast lots and discovered that Yunus (AS) was the cause of their misfortune.

Understanding the gravity of his hasty decision and the consequences of abandoning his mission prematurely, Yunus (AS) chose to sacrifice himself for the safety of the crew. He was thrown overboard into the turbulent sea, where he was swallowed by an immense fish. In the darkness of the fish's belly, Yunus (AS) repented sincerely and sought Allah's forgiveness.

"Allah said, 'Had it not been that he was of those who exalt Allah, he would have remained inside its belly until the Day they are resurrected.'" (Quran, Surah As-Saffat, 37:143-144)

In His boundless mercy, Allah accepted Yunus's (AS) repentance. The fish spat him onto the shore, unharmed. Realizing the gravity of his error, Yunus (AS) returned to his people, who had witnessed the divine intervention. This time, they heeded his message, repented, and turned to Allah in sincere worship.

The story of Prophet Yunus (AS) is a profound lesson in Allah's mercy, the consequences of abandoning one's mission, and the transformative power of repentance. It emphasizes that, no matter how dire the situation, Allah's mercy is vast, and sincere repentance is always met with forgiveness and redemption.

The Prayer of Prophet Zakariya (AS) and the Birth of Yahya (AS)

Prophet Zakariya (AS) stood within the hallowed walls of the House of Worship, his devotion evident in every prostration and supplication. Despite the weight of old age upon his shoulders, his heart remained steadfast in its pursuit of Allah's mercy and guidance.

Yearning for a pious heir to carry forth the mantle of prophethood, Zakariya (AS) immersed himself in prayer, beseeching Allah for an inheritor who would continue the sacred mission of guiding humanity towards righteousness.

In a moment that transcended the boundaries of the physical realm, the angel Jibreel (Gabriel) descended with glad tidings. Allah had heard Zakariya's (AS) plea and decreed the birth of a son, to be named Yahya (AS). Yahya, meaning "John" in English, was destined to be a noble, chaste, and wise prophet.

Zakariya (AS) stood in awe as he received this divine revelation, mindful of his advanced age and his wife's apparent barrenness. Allah, however, gently reminded him that He, the Creator of all things, held the power to bring forth existence with a mere utterance. Filled with gratitude and humility, Zakariya (AS) accepted this miraculous decree.

In due time, Maryam (Mary) bore the miraculous child Yahya (AS), whose upbringing mirrored the righteousness of his father. Yahya's (AS) life unfolded as a testament to the power of sincere prayer, unwavering faith, and the boundless capabilities of Allah.

As Yahya (AS) grew, he embraced his prophetic mission with zeal, calling people to worship the One true God and championing justice and righteousness. The narrative of Prophet Zakariya (AS) and the miraculous birth of Yahya (AS) resonates as a beacon of hope, patience, and divine promise fulfillment—a compelling reminder that nothing lies beyond the reach of Allah's infinite will.

The Miraculous Birth and Prophetic Mission of Isa (AS) in the Quran

In the Quran, the captivating narrative of Prophet Isa (AS), or Jesus in English, unfolds with extraordinary events surrounding his birth. Maryam (Mary), a pious and chaste woman, is divinely chosen by Allah to bear the honorable responsibility of becoming the mother of Isa (AS). One momentous day, while immersed in worship, Maryam is visited by the angel Jibreel (Gabriel), who brings the divine message that she will conceive a child through the command of Allah.

Amidst the challenges of societal scrutiny during her pregnancy, Allah miraculously sustains Maryam with dates and water from a nearby palm tree. When the time for delivery arrives, Maryam seeks refuge in a secluded place and, under the protective shade of a palm tree, brings forth Isa (AS).

As an infant, Isa (AS) astoundingly speaks from the cradle, affirming his prophethood and stressing the importance of monotheism. His divine mission becomes increasingly apparent as he matures. The Quran recounts numerous miracles attributed to Isa (AS), including the healing of the blind and lepers, the raising of the dead, and the crafting of birds from clay, brought to life with the permission of Allah.

Isa (AS) tirelessly advocates for the worship of the One true God and the rejection of associating partners with Allah. He emphasizes that he is not divine but a chosen messenger, appointed to guide the Children of Israel. Despite the undeniable miracles, Isa (AS) faces rejection and a conspiracy against him. In His infinite wisdom, Allah elevates Isa (AS) to the heavens, saving him from the crucifixion that some mistakenly believed would befall him.

The eventual return of Isa (AS) is a promise deeply rooted in Islamic tradition, where he will play a pivotal role in the unfolding events leading up to the Day of Judgment. The story of Prophet Isa (AS) in the Quran serves as a profound reminder of the importance of monotheism, the miraculous nature of Allah's power, and the unwavering steadfastness of His chosen messengers.

As Isa (AS) ascends to the heavens, a sense of anticipation lingers among the believers, awaiting the fulfillment of Allah's promise of his return. The narrative underscores the divine wisdom behind the events surrounding Isa's (AS) life and departure, emphasizing the transcendence of Allah's plan beyond human comprehension.

The period following Isa's (AS) ascent witnesses the continued propagation of his teachings through his disciples, who steadfastly convey the message of monotheism and the worship of the Almighty. Communities embrace the guidance brought by Isa (AS), recognizing the truth in his words and the miracles that accompanied his ministry.

Meanwhile, the followers of Isa (AS) face challenges and persecution from those who resist the monotheistic message. Despite adversities, the faith of the believers remains unshaken, echoing the resilience exemplified by the prophets before them.

The Quranic narrative of Isa (AS) serves as a timeless beacon of inspiration for believers, instilling in them the values of faith, perseverance, and unwavering commitment to the worship of the One true God. It also underscores the concept of divine mercy, as Allah, in His benevolence, grants respite to those who adhere to the righteous path.

As generations pass, the legacy of Isa (AS) endures, and the promise of his eventual return becomes a source of hope for believers facing trials and tribulations. The anticipation of witnessing Isa's (AS) return becomes a driving force for maintaining steadfastness in faith and adherence to the teachings of Islam.

In the broader context of the Quran, the story of Prophet Isa (AS) intertwines with the overarching narrative of divine guidance for humanity. It highlights the interconnectedness of the prophets and their unified message, emphasizing the core principles of monotheism, moral conduct, and compassion toward fellow beings.

Ultimately, the tale of Prophet Isa (AS) in the Quran serves as a testament to the enduring power of divine revelation, offering guidance and solace to believers navigating the complexities of life. It reinforces the timeless truth that, despite the challenges faced by the faithful, Allah's mercy and wisdom prevail, paving the way for the ultimate fulfillment of His divine plan.

Dhul-Qarnayn (AS): The Righteous Sovereign and Explorer of the Farthest Reaches of the Earth

In the Quran, the captivating narrative of Dhul-Qarnayn unfolds within Surah Al-Kahf (18:83-101). Dhul-Qarnayn, translated as "The Two-Horned One," emerges as a paragon of virtue and equity, bestowed with extraordinary strength and sagacity by the grace of Allah. His saga stands as a testament to the supremacy of justice and the unyielding pursuit of righteousness.

Embarking on a noble quest, Dhul-Qarnayn set out to establish justice and disseminate the message of monotheism. His global journey led him through diverse nations, exposing him to a myriad of ways of life. Amidst his travels, Dhul-Qarnayn encountered a people ensnared in the malevolence of Gog and Magog, two unruly and corrupt tribes sowing chaos and oppression.

Moved by the earnest pleas of the beleaguered populace, Dhul-Qarnayn resolved to quell the havoc wrought by Gog and Magog. Armed with divine wisdom and strength, he erected an imposing barrier, meticulously crafted from iron and molten copper. This colossal structure served as a formidable restraint, confining the two tribes to a delimited space and shielding the innocent from their malevolent influence.

Undeterred, Dhul-Qarnayn continued his odyssey, traversing the extremities of the earth and beholding the multifarious creations of Allah. His unwavering dedication to Allah and commitment to justice marked every step of his journey. The Quran extols Dhul-Qarnayn for his righteous deeds, applauding his steadfast adherence to justice and his acknowledgment of the divine guidance that illuminated his path.

The saga of Dhul-Qarnayn underscores the profound significance of justice, wisdom, and the recognition of divine guidance in leadership. It also underscores the notion of exploration and the pursuit of knowledge as a means of comprehending and marveling at the diverse world meticulously crafted by Allah. In embracing these principles, Dhul-Qarnayn left an indelible legacy that continues to inspire seekers of justice and wisdom across the ages.

As Dhul-Qarnayn journeyed further into the uncharted territories, his encounters with different civilizations enriched his understanding of the diverse ways in which people worshiped and lived. He engaged in dialogues with scholars, leaders, and ordinary folk, fostering a climate of mutual respect and understanding. His commitment to justice extended beyond his role as a ruler, transcending cultural and linguistic boundaries.

In one particular city, Dhul-Qarnayn encountered a community grappling with internal strife. Instead of imposing his will, he sought to mediate and reconcile the conflicting parties. Employing his wisdom and divine-guided insight, he facilitated a resolution that brought about harmony and unity. This act of diplomacy and conflict resolution further solidified his reputation as a just and compassionate leader.

Dhul-Qarnayn's explorations led him to breathtaking landscapes, from lush valleys to towering mountains. Along the way, he marveled at the intricate design of Allah's creation. His heart swelled with gratitude, and he frequently engaged in prayer, thanking Allah for the opportunity to witness the beauty and diversity of the Earth.

Despite the challenges he faced, Dhul-Qarnayn remained steadfast in his devotion to Allah. His encounters with various cultures and civilizations reinforced his belief in the universality of the message of monotheism. He tirelessly spread the teachings of Islam, emphasizing the importance of compassion, justice, and humility in the service of Allah.

As he reached the furthest corners of the Earth, Dhul-Qarnayn's expedition became a symbol of the pursuit of knowledge and the exploration of Allah's creation. His legacy lived on in the hearts of those who heard tales of his just rule, wise governance, and unwavering commitment to Allah's guidance.

The story of Dhul-Qarnayn serves as a timeless beacon, inspiring leaders to seek justice, foster understanding among diverse communities, and appreciate the vastness of Allah's creation. His tale echoes through the ages, inviting all to embark on a journey of exploration, both of the world around them and the depths of their own souls.

The Wisdom of Prophet Idris (AS): Keeper of Heavenly Secrets

In the annals of prophethood, the name of Prophet Idris (AS) stands as a testament to wisdom and celestial knowledge. Mentioned briefly in the Quran, Prophet Idris is revered as a man of profound understanding and divine secrets.

Prophet Idris (AS) lived in the era after Prophet Adam (AS) and before Prophet Nuh (AS). His time was marked by a community seeking enlightenment and guidance. Idris (AS), in his dedication to worship and contemplation, was blessed with unique insights into the mysteries of the universe.

Known as a man of few words but immense wisdom, Prophet Idris (AS) would ascend to the heights of mountains, distancing himself from the hustle of daily life. There, in solitude, he engaged in fervent prayers and sought the closeness of Allah.

One of the distinguishing features of Prophet Idris (AS) was his ability to comprehend the intricacies of the heavenly bodies and their movements. Allah granted him the knowledge of astronomy, allowing him to decipher the celestial language written across the skies. Idris (AS) observed the patterns of the stars, the orbits of the planets, and the cosmic ballet that unfolded above.

His wisdom extended beyond the physical realm, encompassing spiritual insights that illuminated the hearts of those who sought his counsel. People from near and far would journey to meet the sage, eager to absorb the divine wisdom that flowed through him.

Prophet Idris (AS) was not only a keeper of celestial secrets but also a guide for his community. He imparted teachings on righteous living, moral conduct, and the worship of the One true God. His gentle demeanor and profound words drew people closer to the path of piety.

While the details of Prophet Idris's life are not extensively documented, the Quran acknowledges his elevated status, mentioning him among the "steadfast" and "truthful" (Quran 19:56-57).

As the keeper of heavenly secrets, Prophet Idris (AS) left an indelible mark on the quest for knowledge and the pursuit of spiritual enlightenment. His legacy echoes through time, reminding believers of the importance of seeking both earthly and celestial wisdom while remaining steadfast in devotion to Allah.

Prophet Idris (AS), known as a sage and keeper of heavenly secrets, continued his solitary endeavors atop the mountains, where he conversed with Allah in moments of deep reflection and contemplation.

One day, as he communed with the Divine, Allah granted Prophet Idris (AS) a unique and sacred gift—the knowledge of writing. This divine script was a form of communication between Idris (AS) and Allah, a medium through which celestial wisdom flowed. With this heavenly script, Prophet Idris (AS) recorded the divine revelations, compiling the knowledge bestowed upon him by Allah.

This sacred knowledge encompassed not only the secrets of the cosmos but also insights into the moral and ethical principles that should govern human conduct. Prophet Idris (AS) meticulously transcribed these divine teachings, creating a legacy that would guide generations to come.

The heavenly script became a source of enlightenment for those who sought to understand the intricacies of creation and the purpose of existence. Prophet Idris (AS) shared this wisdom with his people, encouraging them to reflect on the signs of Allah evident in the world around them.

As a testament to his elevated status, Prophet Idris (AS) became a spiritual leader for his community. People flocked to him, drawn by the magnetism of his wisdom and the divine aura that surrounded him. His teachings resonated with the hearts of those who longed for a deeper connection with the Creator.

Prophet Idris (AS) remained steadfast in his commitment to worship and servitude to Allah. His life exemplified the harmonious balance between the pursuit of knowledge and spiritual devotion. The legacy of Prophet Idris (AS) continued to thrive even after his departure from this world.

While the details of his passing remain veiled in the mysteries of time, the impact of Prophet Idris (AS) endures through the sacred script he left behind—a timeless guide for those who seek wisdom, righteousness, and a profound connection with the Divine.

The story of Prophet Idris (AS) serves as a radiant beacon, illuminating the path of knowledge, spirituality, and unwavering devotion to Allah. His journey stands as a testament to the transformative power of divine wisdom, reminding believers of the infinite possibilities that unfold when the heart is open to the secrets of the heavens.

Prophet Sulaiman (AS): The Gift of Wisdom and Dominion

In the era of divine revelation, there lived a prophet named Sulaiman (AS), known for his exceptional wisdom, piety, and connection with the Almighty. Sulaiman was bestowed with a unique gift from Allah - the gift of wisdom and dominion over the realms of creation.

As the son of Prophet Dawood (AS), Sulaiman inherited the legacy of prophethood and the mantle of kingship. His reign was marked by an extraordinary blend of spiritual insight and earthly sovereignty. His wisdom, often described as unparalleled, was not only a source of guidance for his people but also extended to the natural world.

One of the most renowned accounts of Prophet Sulaiman's wisdom and dominion is the story of the hoopoe bird. One day, Sulaiman noticed the absence of a particular bird from his assembly during a gathering where all creatures were present. Troubled by this, he declared, "I will surely punish the hoopoe severely unless he brings me a clear reason for his absence or presents an excuse."

In response, the hoopoe arrived with news from a distant land, the kingdom of Sheba, ruled by a queen named Bilqis. The bird informed Sulaiman about the queen's people, their customs, and their inclination towards sun worship. Sulaiman, recognizing the opportunity to spread the message of monotheism, decided to send a letter to Bilqis, inviting her and her people to submit to the worship of the one true God.

Sulaiman's letter reached Bilqis, who, intrigued by its content, sought counsel from her advisors. Witnessing the unity and wisdom of Sulaiman's dominion, Bilqis acknowledged the divine message and decided to visit Sulaiman's kingdom.

Upon her arrival, Bilqis was mesmerized by the grandeur and orderliness of Sulaiman's court, which included not only humans but also jinn, birds, and animals, all in harmonious submission to the Prophet's command. Realizing the truth of Sulaiman's message, Bilqis embraced the worship of the one true God, and her people followed suit.

Prophet Sulaiman's gift of wisdom and dominion over the natural and supernatural realms served as a beacon of divine light, illuminating the path of righteousness and monotheism. His reign became a golden era, characterized by justice, compassion, and the worship of the Almighty. The legacy of Prophet Sulaiman (AS) endures as a testament to the profound impact of wisdom guided by divine revelation.

The dominion granted to Prophet Sulaiman (AS) extended beyond the realm of animals and humans to the elements of nature. One of the well-known narratives highlights his remarkable control over the winds, making them subservient to his command. Through this divine gift, Sulaiman could journey swiftly across vast distances, ensuring the efficient governance of his vast kingdom.

Another manifestation of Prophet Sulaiman's wisdom was demonstrated in the famous case of the ants. As his army marched, Sulaiman observed an ant warning its fellow ants to retreat into their dwellings to avoid being unknowingly trampled by the approaching army. Struck by the wisdom and communication within the ant community, Sulaiman smiled, recognizing the intricate balance in the natural order that echoed the harmony he sought to establish in his kingdom.

Despite the immense power and dominion granted to him, Prophet Sulaiman (AS) remained humble and deeply connected to Allah. His wisdom was not wielded for personal gain or pride; instead, it was a tool for justice, compassion, and the propagation of monotheism.

One of the most enduring stories from the life of Prophet Sulaiman is the construction of the grand Temple of Solomon, often referred to as the First Temple. It became a symbol of divine worship, drawing people from various lands to witness the splendor of a structure built in complete submission to Allah's guidance.

The reign of Prophet Sulaiman (AS) became synonymous with an era of unparalleled peace and prosperity. The wisdom granted to him by Allah, coupled with his just governance, left an indelible mark on history. His story continues to inspire believers, emphasizing the importance of seeking wisdom, maintaining humility, and utilizing authority for the betterment of humanity.

The gift of wisdom and dominion bestowed upon Sulaiman (AS) remains a testament to Allah's infinite mercy and the profound impact one individual, guided by divine principles, can have on the course of history. Prophet Sulaiman's legacy serves as a timeless reminder of the transformative power of wisdom and the enduring impact of righteous leadership.

Luqman (AS): Lessons in Wisdom and Parental Guidance

In the ancient lands, nestled among valleys and rolling hills, there lived a man named Luqman known far and wide for his unparalleled wisdom. Although not a prophet, his sagacity rivaled the great scholars of his time.

Luqman's wisdom was not only a gift from Allah but a product of a life well-lived and a heart deeply connected to the divine. His reputation for insight and understanding drew people from distant lands, seeking his counsel in matters of life, faith, and relationships.

One day, as Luqman sat beneath the shade of a large tree, contemplating the wonders of creation, a group of people approached him, eager to glean wisdom from his words. Among them were parents, yearning for guidance in the noble task of raising righteous children.

With a gentle smile, Luqman began to impart his timeless lessons on parental guidance. He emphasized the importance of instilling love and respect for Allah in the hearts of children from a young age. He shared anecdotes from his own life, illustrating the power of leading by example, for actions often speak louder than words.

"O parents," Luqman said, "be mindful of your actions, for your children are keen observers. Let your conduct reflect the values you wish to instill in their hearts. Teach them gratitude, humility, and compassion, for these virtues form the foundation of a righteous character."

Luqman continued, addressing the delicate balance between discipline and compassion. He stressed the significance of correcting children with gentleness, guiding them to understand the consequences of their actions rather than resorting to harshness.

He narrated the story of the Prophet Ibrahim (AS) and his son Isma'il, highlighting the exemplary relationship between a father and a son devoted to Allah. "Embrace the teachings of the prophets," Luqman advised. "Their stories are wellsprings of wisdom for those who seek guidance in the art of parenting."

As the gathering absorbed Luqman's words, they realized that true wisdom lay not only in academic knowledge but in the application of ethical principles in everyday life. Luqman's teachings became a beacon for parents, echoing through generations, and his name became synonymous with wisdom and parental guidance.

And so, under the sprawling tree, Luqman continued to share his insights, leaving an indelible mark on the hearts of those who sought the wisdom of this humble man, a beacon of light in the journey of parenthood.

Luqman's reputation spread far and wide, reaching the ears of a wise and just king who sought his counsel in matters of governance. The king, drawn by the tales of Luqman's profound wisdom, dispatched envoys to invite him to the royal court.

Upon arriving at the grand palace, Luqman was welcomed with honor and respect. The king, eager to learn from this paragon of wisdom, posed questions on matters of leadership, justice, and the intricacies of human nature.

Luqman, with humility befitting his character, shared insights that transcended the temporal realm. He spoke of justice as a cornerstone of leadership, emphasizing the responsibility of rulers to ensure fairness and equity for all subjects. His words echoed the divine guidance found in the Quran and the traditions of the Prophet Muhammad (SAW).

In one poignant exchange, the king asked, "How does one achieve true wisdom?" Luqman, ever humble, replied, "True wisdom comes from acknowledging one's limitations and seeking knowledge with sincerity. It is the ability to recognize the divine order in all things and to tread the path of righteousness."

As Luqman continued to counsel the king, his words resonated not only with the ruler but also with the entire court. His wisdom, rooted in the principles of justice, humility, and devotion to Allah, left an enduring impact on the hearts of those in attendance.

In time, Luqman returned to his humble abode, content to live a life of simplicity and reflection. His wisdom, however, continued to inspire generations, becoming a guiding light for leaders, parents, and seekers of truth.

The legacy of Luqman (AS) endures as a testament to the transformative power of wisdom rooted in faith. His teachings, shared beneath the shade of a tree and within the halls of royalty, exemplify the universal principles that guide humanity toward a life of virtue, understanding, and devotion to the divine.

Made in the USA
Monee, IL
12 November 2024

69972262R00044